Intuitive-Keep Moving-The best is yet to come

Lizette

Published by Lizette, 2024.

INTUITIVE-KEEP MOVING-THE BEST IS YET TO COME

First edition. June 28, 2024.

ISBN: 979-8227870407

Written by Lizette.

Intuitive

"KEEP MOVING,

      the best is yet to come".

1

Lizette

Intuitive-Keep moving, the best is yet to come!
Author Lizette Theron

First Edition

Dedicated to Jessica and Rebecca.
Author Lizette

I grew up in South Africa and love being in nature and i have 2 grown up daughters and a wonderful husband that supports me emotionally and while i was going through my own trauma. And so i wrote this to help those in pain navigate and have some tools of their own for the healing journey. From my trauma i learned to navigate my own path of healing and heal myself by using a lot of natural tools to see the kaleidoscope of life and i just always remembered to move through all the pain and see suffering as growth and still navigate the journey of life.
Quotes from the book "Eat Pray Love"

"When the past has passed from you at last, let go. Then climb down and begin the rest of your life. With great joy"

"When the karma of a relationship is done, only love remains. It's safe. Let go"

"This is a good sign, having a broken heart.It means we have tried for something.

"If you clear out all of that space in your mind you would have a door way."

Chapter 1

Growing your Intuition for a Growth Mindset

Growing your intuition for a growth mindset involves cultivating several key habits and practices:

Embrace Challenges: Rather than shying away from difficult tasks, see them as opportunities for growth. Approach challenges with a mindset of curiosity and determination to learn and improve.

Learn from Failures: Instead of viewing failure as a setback, see it as a valuable learning experience. Analyze what went wrong, extract lessons from it, and use that knowledge to adjust your approach going forward.

Maintain a Positive Attitude: Cultivate optimism and resilience in the face of obstacles. Focus on what you can control and remain hopeful about your ability to overcome challenges.

Seek Feedback: Be open to feedback from others and use it as an opportunity to learn and grow. Constructive criticism can provide valuable insights and help you identify areas for improvement.

Persist in the Face of Adversity: Develop perseverance and determination to keep moving forward, even when the going gets tough. Stay committed to your goals and believe in your ability to succeed despite setbacks.

Embrace Learning: Adopt a mindset of continuous learning and growth. Be curious about new ideas, perspectives, and experiences, and actively seek out opportunities for personal and professional development.

Cultivate Self-Awareness: Reflect on your thoughts, feelings, and behaviors to gain insight into your strengths, weaknesses, and areas for growth. Self-awareness allows you to make more informed decisions and take proactive steps toward self-improvement.

Practice Mindfulness: Cultivate mindfulness practices such as meditation, deep breathing, or mindfulness exercises to become more present and aware of your thoughts and emotions. Mindfulness can help you tune into your intuition and make decisions aligned with your values and goals.

By incorporating these habits into your daily life, you can nurture your intuition for a growth mindset and create a foundation for personal and professional development.

Chapter 2

Growth Mindset Versus Fixed Mindset

Growth mindset versus fixed mindset.

It is a belief that one's abilities and

intelligence can be developed and improved over time with effort,

learning, and perseverance.

Here are some key principles of a growth mindset:

• Embracing challenges- see it as a opportunity to learn and grow instead of avoiding difficult tasks, welcome it as a

chance to developnew skills.

• Persistence in the face of setbacks-dont be discouraged by failure

but rather see it as a stepping stone to

success and motivate yourself to try again.

• Effort is a path-putting in hard work is a key to mastering a skill

or achieving a goal and continious effort
leads to improvement.

• Learn from constructive feedback and see it as valuable imput for
growth and identify areas for improvement
after criticism and dont take it personally.

• Inspire yourself by the success of others and dont feel threatened
and see it as inspiration to work towards your own goals.

• Try and cultivate a love for learning and development and expand

your knowledge and develop new skills.

• Never say never just say not yet but i will

get there and perseverance.

• Be flexible and try new approaches and if something doesnt work
adjust and adapt and there are many different paths to success
• Celebrate every little milestone.
• It is a lifelong journey and enjoy the ride and try and cultivate

your new approach.

Chapter 3 Limiting Beliefs

Cultivating a Growth Mindset

Addressing limiting beliefs is a crucial aspect of cultivating a growth mindset.

Here's how you can approach it:

Identify Limiting Beliefs: Begin by becoming aware of the beliefs that may be holding you back. These beliefs often manifest as self-doubt, fear of failure, or negative self-talk. Pay attention to the thoughts that arise when you face challenges or setbacks.

Challenge Your Beliefs: Once you've identified limiting beliefs, question their validity. Ask yourself if there is evidence to support these beliefs or if they are based on assumptions or past experiences. Challenge the negative thoughts with more realistic and empowering alternatives.

Reframe Negative Thoughts: Reframe negative thoughts into more positive and empowering ones. Instead of saying "I can't do this," try saying "I haven't figured it out yet." Focus on the potential for growth and learning inherent in every situation.

Practice Self-Compassion: Be kind and compassionate toward yourself, especially when facing challenges or setbacks. Recognize that everyone experiences moments of doubt and failure, and that it's part of the learning process. Treat yourself with the same kindness and understanding that you would offer to a friend.

Set Realistic Goals: Break down your goals into smaller, manageable steps and celebrate your progress along the way. Setting realistic goals helps build confidence and reinforces the belief that progress is possible.

Visualize Success: Use visualization techniques to imagine yourself succeeding and overcoming obstacles. Visualizing success can help reinforce positive beliefs and increase confidence in your abilities.

Seek Support: Surround yourself with supportive and positive influences. Seek out mentors, coaches, or friends who can offer encouragement and help challenge your limiting beliefs.

Take Action: Finally, take proactive steps to challenge your limiting beliefs by stepping outside of your comfort zone and trying new things. Each small success will help build confidence and chip away at negative beliefs.

Limiting Beliefs

I want to avoid making mistakes
I give up

This is not good enough

Il never be that smart

By actively challenging and reframing limiting beliefs, you can create a mindset that is more conducive to growth and success. Remember that change takes time and effort, but with persistence and dedication, you can cultivate a more empowering belief system.

Chapter 4

Building Resilience while Working Towards a Growth Mindset

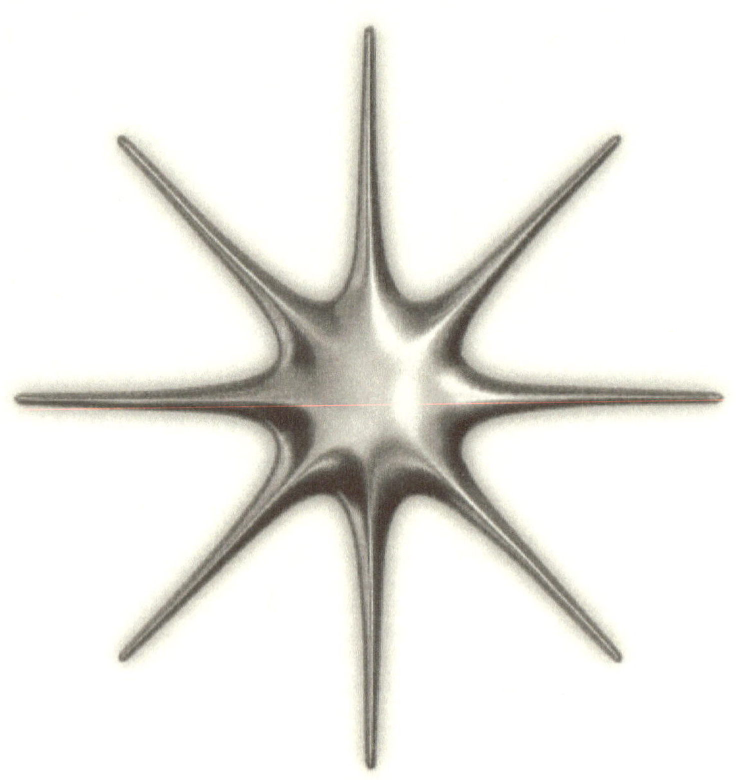

Building resilience while working towards a growth mindset is essential for navigating the challenges and setbacks that inevitably arise on the path to personal and professional growth. Here's how you can develop resilience alongside fostering a growth mindset:

Cultivate Self-Awareness: Start by becoming aware of your thoughts, emotions, and reactions to challenging situations. Recognize when you're facing adversity and acknowledge your feelings without judgment. Self-awareness is the first step towards building resilience.

Practice Optimism: Foster a positive outlook by focusing on opportunities rather than obstacles. Train yourself to see setbacks as temporary and solvable challenges rather than insurmountable problems. Optimism can help you bounce back more quickly from adversity.

Develop Problem-Solving Skills: Enhance your ability to cope with challenges by developing effective problem-solving skills.

Break down problems into smaller, more manageable parts and brainstorm possible solutions. Having a proactive approach to problem-solving can increase your resilience in the face of adversity.

Build a Support System: Surround yourself with a supportive network of friends, family, mentors, and colleagues who can offer encouragement, advice, and assistance during difficult times. Having a strong support system can provide emotional support and practical help when you need it most.

Practice Self-Care: Take care of your physical, emotional, and mental well-being by prioritizing self-care activities such as exercise, healthy eating, adequate sleep, relaxation techniques, and mindfulness practices. Taking care of yourself enhances your resilience and ability to cope with stress.

Embrace Failure as a Learning Opportunity: Adopt a growth mindset by viewing failures and setbacks as opportunities for learning and growth. Instead of dwelling on mistakes, extract valuable lessons from them and use that knowledge to improve and adapt your approach in the future.

Set Realistic Goals: Establish achievable goals that stretch your abilities but are still within reach. Break down larger goals into smaller, actionable steps and celebrate your progress along the way. Setting realistic goals helps prevent burnout and fosters a sense of accomplishment.

Maintain Flexibility: Be willing to adapt and adjust your plans when faced with unexpected challenges or changes.

Flexibility allows you to navigate obstacles more effectively and find alternative solutions when necessary.

Practice Resilience-Building Exercises: Engage in activities that promote resilience, such as journaling, gratitude practices, visualization exercises, and mindfulness meditation. These practices can help you build mental toughness and emotional resilience over time.

By integrating these strategies into your daily life, you can develop both resilience and a growth mindset, enabling you to thrive in the face of adversity and pursue your goals with confidence and determination.

Building resilience

Develop a support structure from your relationships with friends and
family, colleagues or support groups, talk
about your feelings and experiences. Dont hesitate to reach out to
a health professional if
you need additional support.

Focus on what you can control and look for the lesson.
Practice gratitude and acknowledge the positive aspects of your life

Promote self-care and ensure you get enough sleep, eat well, and

exercise, something you enjoy doing as well like meditation,
yoga and promote emotional well-being.

Try and engage in activities that bring you joy and serve as a healthy
outlet for stress.
brace adaptibility and view challenges as growth.

Chapter 5 Approaches to a Growth Mindset

Approaching a growth mindset involves adopting a specific attitude and set of behaviors that prioritize learning, development, and resilience. Here's how you can cultivate and embrace a growth mindset:

Believe in the Power of Growth: Embrace the belief that your abilities and intelligence can be developed through dedication, effort, and perseverance.

Recognize that talent and intelligence are not fixed traits but can be cultivated and improved over time.

View Challenges as Opportunities: Instead of avoiding challenges, see them as opportunities for growth and learning.

Embrace new experiences and tasks that push you out of your comfort zone, knowing that they will help you develop new skills and abilities.

Learn from Failure: Embrace failure as a natural part of the learning process rather than a sign of incompetence. Understand that setbacks and mistakes are opportunities to learn, grow, and improve.

Analyze what went wrong, extract valuable lessons from the experience, and use that knowledge to inform your future actions.

Persist in the Face of Adversity: Develop resilience and perseverance in pursuing your goals, even when faced with obstacles or setbacks. Stay committed to your objectives and maintain a positive attitude, knowing that setbacks are temporary and can be overcome with effort and determination.

Embrace Effort: Value the process of learning and growth over the pursuit of immediate success. Embrace effort as a necessary component of achievement and understand that mastery requires consistent practice, hard work, and dedication.

Seek Feedback and Criticism: Be open to feedback from others and use it as an opportunity to learn and improve. View constructive criticism as valuable input for growth rather than a personal attack. Actively seek out feedback from mentors, peers, and colleagues to gain new perspectives and insights.

Celebrate Growth and Progress: Acknowledge and celebrate your progress and achievements, no matter how small.

Take pride in your efforts and the improvements you've made along the way. Cultivate a sense of accomplishment and satisfaction in the process of learning and development.

Cultivate Curiosity: Foster a sense of curiosity and a desire to learn new things. Stay curious about the world around you and actively seek out opportunities for exploration and discovery. Approach challenges with a sense of curiosity and a willingness to experiment and try new approaches.

By adopting these attitudes and behaviors, you can cultivate a growth mindset that empowers you to embrace challenges, learn from failure, and continuously strive for improvement and success.

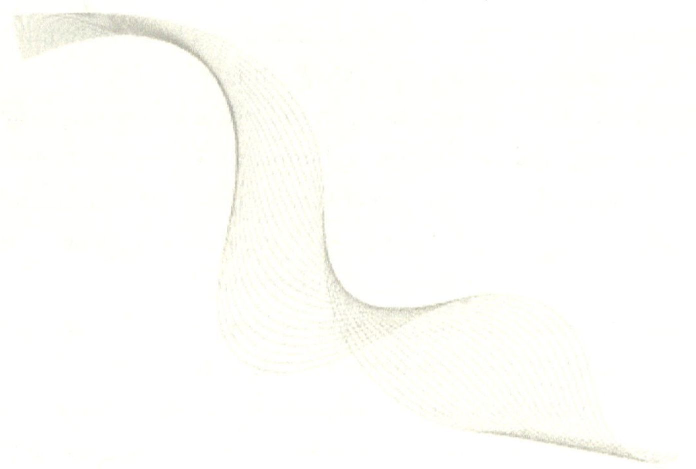

Develop grit-stay committed to long term goals despite setbacks,
obstacles and failures.
Practice resilience-Bounce back from setbacks and use them as learning
experiences.
Value your effort over outcome and focus on process.

Stay curious and open to new ideas, knowledge and skill

Develop your own strategies to overcome obstacles.

Use positive self-talk like positive affirmations.
Choose a support structure that creates
growth and learning and collaborative approach.

Recognize your strengths and resilience in action and try see things

in a balanced and realistic light.

Laugh a lot and connect with your core values and beliefs and it will
give you a sense of purpose and direction.
Help others by volunteering and learn to
say no when you cant and dontfeel guilty.

Chapter 6

objectives of a Growth Mindset Versus Fixed Mindset

The objectives of a growth mindset and a fixed mindset differ significantly, as they reflect distinct attitudes and approaches towards learning, challenges, and personal development.

Objectives of a Growth Mindset:

Embrace Challenges: The primary objective of a growth mindset is to see challenges as opportunities for growth and learning. Individuals with a growth mindset actively seek out challenges and view setbacks as temporary obstacles that can be overcome with effort and perseverance.
Learn from Failure: In a growth mindset, the objective is to learn from failure rather than avoid it. Individuals with a growth mindset understand that setbacks are a natural part of the learning process and use them as opportunities to reflect, adapt, and improve.
Cultivate Resilience: Building resilience is a key objective of a growth mindset.
Individuals with this mindset approach adversity with a sense of optimism and perseverance, knowing that they have the ability to bounce back and overcome obstacles.
Value Effort and Persistence: In a growth mindset, the objective is to prioritize effort and persistence over innate talent or ability. Individuals focus on the process of learning and development, understanding that mastery requires consistent practice and dedication.
Seek Feedback and Criticism: The objective of seeking feedback and criticism is to foster growth and improvement.

Individuals with a growth mindset actively seek out feedback from others and use it as a tool for self-reflection and development.

Celebrate Growth and Progress: In a growth mindset, the objective is to celebrate growth and progress, no matter how small. Individuals take pride in their efforts and achievements, recognizing that every step forward is a sign of personal growth and development.

Objectives of a Fixed Mindset:

Avoid Challenges: The primary objective of a fixed mindset is to avoid challenges and situations that may threaten one's sense of competence. Individuals with a fixed mindset may shy away from difficult tasks or situations where they feel they may not succeed.

Fear Failure: In a fixed mindset, the objective is to avoid failure at all costs. Individuals may perceive failure as a reflection of their inherent abilities or intelligence, leading them to avoid taking risks or trying new things.

Maintain Comfort and Security: The objective of a fixed mindset is to maintain a sense of comfort and security by sticking to what is familiar and predictable.

Individuals may resist change and avoid stepping outside of their comfort zones, fearing the unknown.

Rely on Natural Talent: In a fixed mindset, the objective is to rely on innate talent or ability rather than effort or persistence. Individuals may believe that their abilities are fixed and immutable, leading them to attribute success or failure solely to their inherent traits.

Avoid Feedback and Criticism: The objective of avoiding feedback and criticism is to protect one's self-esteem and sense of worth. Individuals with a fixed mindset may be reluctant to seek out feedback from others or may reject criticism as a personal attack.

Focus on Validation: In a fixed mindset, the objective is to seek external validation and approval rather than focusing on personal growth and development. Individuals may prioritize achievements and accolades as measures of their worth, seeking validation from others rather than from within.

Overall, the objectives of a growth mindset are centered around learning, development, and resilience, while the objectives of a fixed mindset are focused on maintaining comfort, avoiding failure, and seeking external validation.

Objectives of a growth mindset

A growth mindset is the belief that you can improve your abilities and

skills through effort and feedback and learning.

It is opposed to a fixed mindset, which assumes that your talents are

innate. Developing a growth mindset can help you overcome challenges, embrace opportunities and achieve your goals, transform your beliefs
and positively influence behaviour and gain new knowledge.

Chapter 7

Embracing Challenges by Achieving a Growth Mindset

Embracing challenges is a central aspect of achieving a growth mindset. Here's how to approach challenges with a growth mindset:
See Challenges as Opportunities: Instead of viewing challenges as daunting obstacles, see them as opportunities for growth and learning. Recognize that overcoming challenges can help you develop new skills, knowledge, and resilience.
Welcome Discomfort: Embrace discomfort and uncertainty as signs that you're pushing yourself outside of your comfort zone. Understand that growth occurs when you're willing to take risks and confront unfamiliar situations.
Focus on Effort and Learning: Shift your focus from outcomes to the process of learning and improvement. Emphasize the effort you put in and the lessons you gain from facing challenges, rather than solely on achieving a specific result.

Learn from Failure: Embrace failure as a natural part of the learning process.
Understand that setbacks and mistakes provide valuable opportunities for reflection, adjustment, and growth. Use failure as a stepping stone toward future success.
Set Stretch Goals: Set goals that challenge you to stretch beyond your current abilities. Break larger goals down into smaller, manageable steps, and celebrate progress along the way. Aim for continuous improvement rather than perfection.

Seek Feedback and Support: Be open to feedback from others and seek support when facing challenges. Reach out to mentors, peers, or experts who can offer guidance, advice, and encouragement. Use feedback as a tool for learning and growth.

Cultivate Resilience: Develop resilience by maintaining a positive attitude and perseverance in the face of adversity. Stay resilient by reframing setbacks as temporary setbacks rather than permanent failures. Focus on what you can control and adapt your approach as needed.

Celebrate Progress: Celebrate your achievements and milestones, no matter how small. Acknowledge the progress you've made and the lessons you've learned along the way. Cultivate a sense of pride in your growth and development.

By embracing challenges with a growth mindset, you can transform obstacles into opportunities for personal and professional growth. Remember that developing a growth mindset is an ongoing journey that requires practice, patience, and perseverance.

Embracing Challenges
Benefits of embracing challenges Facing fears head-on helps you develop

resilience-the ability to bounce back from setbacks stronger then before. Conquering fears and challenges can lead to a profound sense of accomplishment, which in turn boosts self- confidence and self-esteem. Start small and begin with smaller challenges and work your way up. Celebrate your achievements.

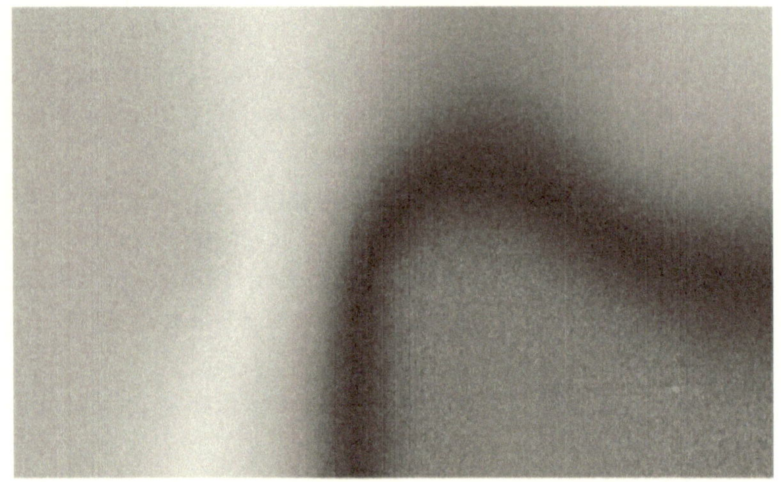

Chapter 8

Tools to Help you Grow in a Growth Mindset Versus Stagnation

Tools to help you grow in a growth mindset versus stagnation can include various strategies, resources, and practices that foster learning, development, and resilience. Here are some tools for each:

Tools for Growing in a Growth Mindset:

Self-Reflection Journals: Maintain a journal to reflect on your experiences, challenges, and growth. Write about your achievements, setbacks, and the lessons you've learned along the way. Use journaling as a tool for self-awareness and personal growth.

Goal Setting Apps: Use goal-setting apps to set, track, and manage your goals. Break down larger goals into smaller, actionable steps and monitor your progress over time.

Goal-setting apps can help you stay focused, motivated, and accountable.

Online Courses and Workshops: Enroll in online courses and workshops to acquire new skills, knowledge, and perspectives. Platforms like Coursera, Udemy, and Khan Academy offer a wide range of courses on various topics, allowing you to pursue continuous learning and development.

Books on Personal Growth: Read books on personal growth, resilience, and mindset to expand your understanding and perspective. Look for titles by authors such as Carol Dweck, Angela Duckworth, and Brené Brown, who offer valuable insights and strategies for cultivating a growth mindset.

Mindfulness and Meditation Apps: Practice mindfulness and meditation using apps like Headspace, Calm, or Insight Timer.

Mindfulness practices can help you develop greater self-awareness, emotional resilience, and focus, supporting your growth mindset journey.

Peer Support Groups: Join peer support groups or communities focused on personal development and growth.

Connect with like-minded individuals who share similar goals and aspirations, and support each other on your respective journeys.

Feedback and Assessment Tools: Seek feedback from peers, mentors, or coaches using assessment tools like 360-degree feedback surveys or personality assessments. Use feedback as a tool for self-awareness and growth, identifying areas for improvement and development.

Tools for Overcoming Stagnation:

Challenge Your Comfort Zone: Use tools like the "Comfort Zone Crusher" worksheet or apps like "Growth Zone" to identify and challenge your comfort zone. Set small, achievable challenges that push you outside of your usual routine and comfort level.

Time Management Apps: Use time management apps like Trello, Asana, or Todoist to organize your tasks and priorities. Set deadlines, create schedules, and track your progress to avoid procrastination and stay focused on your goals.

Accountability Partnerships: Pair up with an accountability partner or join an accountability group to help you stay accountable for your actions and commitments. Share your goals, progress, and challenges with your partner, and provide mutual support and encouragement.

Limiting Belief Worksheets: Use worksheets or exercises designed to identify and challenge limiting beliefs. Tools like the "Belief Inventory Worksheet" or "Limiting Belief Buster" can help you uncover and reframe negative beliefs that may be holding you back.

Stagnation Reflection Questions: Reflect on stagnation using prompts and questions designed to stimulate self-awareness and insight. Ask yourself questions like "What am I avoiding?" or "What am I afraid of?" to uncover underlying barriers to growth and change.

Visualize Your Future Self: Use visualization techniques to imagine your future self and the life you want to create. Visualization exercises can help you clarify your goals, motivations, and aspirations, inspiring you to take action and overcome stagnation.

Personal Development Plans: Create a personal development plan outlining your goals, action steps, and timelines for growth. Use templates or online tools to structure your plan and track your progress over time.

Tools to help

Define your objective areas and what are your existing knowledge and skills. What are your strengths and weaknesses? What is your passions. What skills would you want to develop further and read books , attend webinars and keep journalling. Try new hobbies that you have always wanted to do. Engage with other professionals in your field. Reflect on your past experiences and learn from it and see it in a new way. Be open to new ideas. Walk in nature and observe the spiral of life where ever you find yourself, a spiders web, a flock of birds and frogs in a pond. Observe your pets and weather patterns. Observe your own seasons of life. Your relationships and when to self perserve to growth and then go out.

Chapter 9

Making Goals for Yourself
in a Growth Mindset Versus Limited Mindset

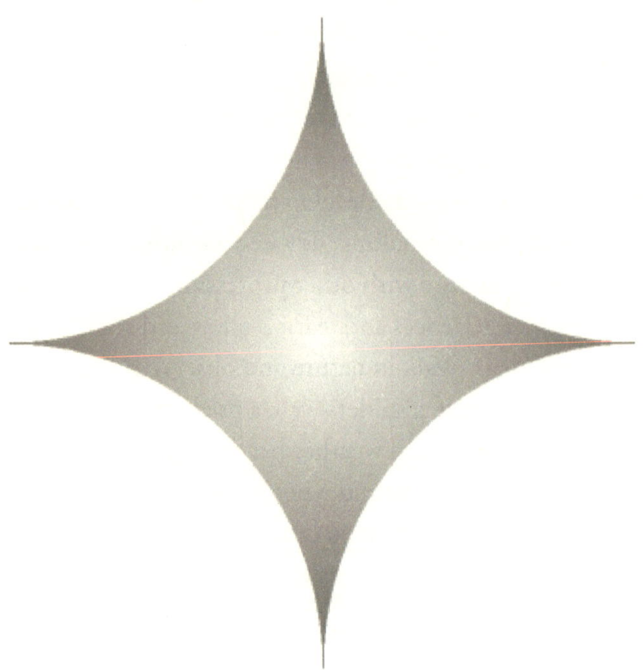

Setting goals in a growth mindset versus a limited mindset involves
approaching goal- setting with different attitudes and perspectives.
Here's how the two mindsets differ in the context of goal-setting:
Goals in a Growth Mindset:
Focus on Learning and Development: Goals set in a growth mindset
prioritize learning, development, and continuous improvement.

Instead of aiming for a specific outcome or achievement, the focus is on the process of growth and mastery.

Embrace Challenges: Goals are designed to stretch your abilities and challenge you to step outside of your comfort zone.

Embracing challenges is seen as an opportunity for growth and learning, rather than a threat to one's competence.

View Failure as Feedback: Failure is seen as a natural part of the learning process and an opportunity for feedback and growth. Goals are set with the understanding that setbacks and mistakes are inevitable but can provide valuable lessons and insights for improvement.

Set Stretch Goals: Goals in a growth mindset are often ambitious and stretch beyond current capabilities. They are designed to inspire and motivate you to reach for new heights and push beyond perceived limitations.

Value Effort and Persistence: Effort and persistence are prioritized over innate talent or ability. Goals are pursued with a strong work ethic and determination, knowing that success is the result of consistent effort and perseverance.

Seek Feedback and Support: Feedback from others is actively sought out and valued as a means of learning and improvement. Goals are set with the understanding that feedback from mentors, peers, and colleagues can provide valuable insights and perspectives.

Goals in a Limited Mindset:

Focus on Avoiding Failure: Goals set in a limited mindset are often focused on avoiding failure or looking good in the eyes of others. The emphasis is on maintaining the status quo and avoiding risks or challenges that may lead to failure.

Avoid Challenges: Goals are set with the intention of staying within one's comfort zone and avoiding situations that may be perceived as difficult or threatening.

Challenges are seen as obstacles to be avoided rather than opportunities for growth.

Fear Failure: Failure is feared and avoided at all costs, as it is seen as a reflection of one's inherent abilities or intelligence.

Goals may be set conservatively to minimize the risk of failure, even if it means sacrificing potential growth and development.
Rely on Fixed Abilities: Goals are set based on existing skills and abilities, with little emphasis on growth or improvement.
There is a belief that talent and intelligence are fixed traits, and success is largely determined by innate abilities rather than effort or learning.
Avoid Feedback and Criticism: Feedback and criticism are often perceived as threats to one's self-esteem or worth. Goals may be pursued in isolation, with little input or feedback from others, to avoid the possibility of criticism or rejection.

Goals

Set yourself small challenges to overcome and reach goals in that way. Take it day by day and dont be hard on yourself. See with a open mind and even if it takes longer to reach a goal, it is ok to start over when ever you want to and achieve it. The accomplishment is refreshing for your brain even if it took longer and forgiveness for self is important. What is perfection but a stigma we grew up with. We are more then enough in every way. Reflection on your current state is ok. Learn from it and move on, the sun always rises no matter what. The tortoise also keeps on moving forward. Just keep moving at your own pace to your goal and the goals can even change from time to time and it is still called moving forward to a growth mindset.

Chapter 10

Sustaining a Growth Mindset

Sustaining a growth mindset in the outside world involves intentional practices and strategies to foster a belief in your ability to grow, learn and improve. So embrace your challenges head on and see it as opportunities for growth rather then obstacles. Seek out new experiences and situations that push you out of your comfort zone. Focus on the process of learning and improving, rather then solely on the outcome. See setbacks as learning experiences rather then failures. Analyze what went wrong and what you can do differently next time. Understand that mistakes are a natural part of the learning process. Break larger goals into smaller achievable ones. Cultivate a positive attitude and practice self compassion and self kindness and focus on your strengths and past successes when faced with challenges. Stay curious and open your mind to new knowledge and skils. Believe in your ability for challenges.

Remember past experiences where you have overcome difficulties. Practice mindfulness and recognize the effort and hard work you put into your growth. Share your success with others to inspire and motivate them. Stay updated with research and articles on personal development and growth. Seek mentors and engage in communities that promote learning and development

then go out. With every revolution we shed old parts of our self and evolve as a more authentic person. We observe light and dark, rest, joy, sorrow.

Life is a spiral and it twists and turns and is ever changing and we must seek harmony honoring the highs and lows and the challenges and blessings. Dance with the rhythm and grow. Art is a form of therapy and growth through learning about the hidden message in your body about what happened in your journey and we all have our own story. So paint your story or write your story. Advocate for your story to help others on their path and love your story and embrace it and so much healing will come from that. Meet other people with stories similar to yours and develop a support network.

People will give you feedback that you can grow from. Walking and hiking teaches you about ups and downs, sand and water teach you about the eb and flow of life and grounding and moving and changing. Rain teaches you about the tears are cleansing and washing away old beliefs. Storms teach you to hold on everything will blow over and the sun will rise again and it will be a new day. Darkness at night teach us about the dark night of the soul and to embrace our inner demons and work through all the darkness to become the butterfly in the sun we were meant to be and be free.

Chapter 11

Be a Changemaker While Having a Growth Mindset

Being a changemaker with a growth mindset involves a combination of proactive behaviors, attitudes, and strategies that drive personal and social transformation. Here are some key principles and actionable steps to embody this role:

Embrace Continuous Learning Cultivate Curiosity:

Always ask questions and seek new information.

Stay updated with the latest trends and research in your field.

Read books, attend workshops, and take courses to expand your knowledge.

Becoming a changemaker with a growth mindset involves adopting a specific set of attitudes, behaviors, and strategies that empower you to drive positive change in your community or the world. Here's how you can cultivate a growth mindset and become a changemaker:

Embrace a Growth Mindset: Cultivate a belief in your ability to grow, learn, and adapt. See challenges as opportunities for growth and view failure as a natural part of the learning process. Embrace a mindset of continuous improvement and strive to develop your skills, knowledge, and abilities over time.

Identify Your Passion and Purpose: Reflect on your values, interests, and passions to identify causes or issues that resonate with you deeply. Clarify your purpose and the impact you want to make in the world. Align your goals and actions with your passion and purpose to drive meaningful change.

Set Ambitious Goals: Set ambitious but achievable goals that align with your vision for change. Break down larger goals into smaller, actionable steps and create a roadmap for achieving them. Set deadlines and milestones to track your progress and stay focused on your objectives.

Seek Opportunities for Learning and Growth: Be proactive in seeking out opportunities for learning and skill development. Take courses, attend workshops, and seek out mentors who can provide guidance and support.

Continuously expand your knowledge and expertise to enhance your effectiveness as a changemaker.

Build Relationships and Collaborate: Cultivate relationships with like-minded individuals, organizations, and communities who share your passion for change. Collaborate with others to amplify your impact and leverage collective resources, expertise, and networks. Foster a sense of community and collaboration to drive positive change together.

Be Adaptive and Resilient: Be open to feedback, adapt to changing circumstances, and persevere in the face of setbacks and challenges. Approach obstacles as opportunities for learning and growth, and maintain a positive attitude even in the face of adversity. Cultivate resilience and tenacity to overcome obstacles and achieve your goals.

Take Action: Take decisive action to turn your vision for change into reality. Start small and build momentum over time. Be proactive in identifying opportunities to make a difference and take initiative to address them. Use your skills, resources, and influence to drive positive change in your community or the world.

Reflect and Iterate: Regularly reflect on your progress, successes, and challenges. Celebrate your achievements and learn from your failures. Use feedback from others and your own experiences to refine your approach and strategies.

Continuously iterate and improve your efforts to maximize your impact as a changemaker.

By adopting a growth mindset and taking purposeful action, you can become a changemaker who drives positive change and makes a meaningful difference in the world.

Chapter 12

Learn from Failures by Having a Growth Mindset

With a growth mindset, failures are seen as opportunities for learning, growth, and improvement. Here are some valuable lessons you can learn from failures when approaching them with a growth mindset: Identify Areas for Improvement: Failure provides valuable feedback on areas where you may need to improve or develop your skills, knowledge, or strategies. By analyzing what went wrong, you can identify specific areas for growth and take proactive steps to address them.

Develop Resilience: Failure can help you build resilience and mental toughness. Embracing failure as a natural part of the learning process teaches you to bounce back from setbacks, persevere in the face of adversity, and maintain a positive attitude despite challenges.

Refine Strategies and Approaches: Failure offers insights into what strategies and approaches may not be effective in achieving your goals. By learning from failure, you can refine your strategies, experiment with new approaches, and adapt your methods to increase your chances of success.

Gain Self-Awareness: Failure provides an opportunity for self-reflection and self- awareness. By examining your thoughts, behaviors, and actions leading up to the failure, you can gain insights into your strengths, weaknesses, and areas for personal growth.

Build Confidence: Overcoming failure builds confidence and self-efficacy. Each time you navigate through failure and emerge stronger on the other side, you reinforce your belief in your ability to overcome challenges and achieve your goals.

Foster a Growth Mindset: Failure reinforces the importance of having a growth mindset. Embracing failure as a learning opportunity and believing in your capacity to grow and improve over time cultivates a mindset of resilience, perseverance, and continuous learning.

Cultivate Adaptability: Failure teaches you to be adaptable and flexible in response to changing circumstances. By learning from failure, you become more adept at adjusting your plans, strategies, and goals to better align with your evolving circumstances and objectives.

Inspire Innovation: Failure encourages innovation and creativity by challenging you to think outside the box and explore new possibilities. By embracing failure as an opportunity for innovation, you can uncover unconventional solutions and approaches that lead to breakthroughs and success.

Learn from Failure:

View setbacks as learning opportunities. Reflect on what went wrong and how to improve in the future.

Encourage a culture where mistakes are seen as part of the growth process.

Foster Innovation and Creativity Think Outside the Box: Challenge the status quo and conventional thinking.

Brainstorm regularly and encourage creative problem-solving techniques like mind mapping or design thinking.

Overall, failure is a powerful teacher that can provide valuable insights, strengthen your resilience, and fuel your growth and development when approached with a growth mindset. By learning from failure, you can turn setbacks into stepping stones for success and continue progressing toward your goals with confidence and determination.

Chapter 13
Inspire Others with Your Growth Mindset

Collaborate with Diverse Teams:
Engage with people from different backgrounds and disciplines.
Value diverse perspectives and leverage them to come up with
innovative solutions.
Develop Resilience and Adaptability Embrace Change:

Be open to change and flexible in your approach.
Adapt quickly to new situations and pivot strategies when necessary.
Build Emotional Resilience:
Practice mindfulness and stress- management techniques.
Maintain a positive attitude, even in the face of challenges.

Drive Impactful Change Identify Key Issues:
Focus on problems that align with your passions and values.
Conduct thorough research to understand the root causes and potential solutions.
Take Initiative:
Be proactive in implementing solutions, even if they are small steps initially.
Mobilize resources and build a support network to amplify your efforts.
Measure and Reflect:
Set clear, measurable goals for your initiatives.
Regularly assess the impact of your actions and adjust strategies accordingly

Inspire and Lead Others Lead by Example:
Demonstrate the behaviors and values you wish to see in others.
Show commitment and integrity in all your actions.
Mentor and Empower:
Support the growth and development of others.
Provide guidance, encouragement, and resources to help others achieve their potential.
Cultivate a Growth-Oriented Environment Encourage Experimentation:
Create a safe space for experimentation and innovation.

Recognize and celebrate efforts and progress, not just successes.
Promote Lifelong Learning:
Offer opportunities for continuous learning and professional development.
Foster a culture where feedback is welcomed and used constructively.
Practical Steps to Implement These Principles
Set Personal Goals:
Define clear, attainable objectives for your personal growth and changemaking efforts.
Break down these goals into actionable steps and track your progress.
Join or Form Communities:
Engage with communities or networks that are focused on similar causes.
Collaborate, share resources, and support each other's initiatives.

Stay Informed and Connected:

Follow thought leaders and organizations in your area of interest.
Attend events, webinars, and conferences to stay informed and network with like- minded individuals.
By integrating these principles and actions into your daily life, you can be a changemaker who not only strives for personal growth but also creates meaningful, positive change in the world around you.

Chapter 14

Living Life Abundantly While Cultivating a Growth Mindset

Living life abundantly while cultivating a growth mindset involves embracing a fulfilling, joyful, and purposeful lifestyle, while continuously seeking personal and professional development. Here's how you can achieve this balance:

Embrace a Positive Mindset Practice Gratitude:

Keep a gratitude journal and write down things you are thankful for daily.
Reflect on positive experiences and celebrate small wins.
Focus on Strengths:
Identify and leverage your unique talents and strengths.
Engage in activities that bring you joy and fulfillment.

Pursue Continuous Learning Set Learning Goals:
Establish clear, specific goals for acquiring new knowledge or skills.
Allocate regular time for learning activities such as reading, online courses, or workshops.
Seek Feedback and Reflect:
Request feedback from peers, mentors, and colleagues to identify areas for improvement.
Reflect on your experiences and learn from both successes and failures.
Foster Meaningful Relationships Build a Supportive Network:
Surround yourself with positive, like- minded individuals who encourage growth and well-being.
Participate in community groups, professional networks, or social clubs.
Practice Empathy and Kindness:
Show genuine interest in others' lives and support their aspirations.
Engage in acts of kindness and contribute to the well-being of your community.
Cultivate Wellness and Balance Prioritize Physical Health:
Maintain a balanced diet, regular exercise, and sufficient sleep.
Engage in physical activities that you enjoy, such as sports, hiking, or dancing
Nurture Mental and Emotional Health:
Practice mindfulness, meditation, or yoga to manage stress and enhance mental clarity.
Set aside time for relaxation and hobbies that rejuvenate your spirit.
Pursue Purpose and Passion Identify Your Purpose:
Reflect on what truly matters to you and what impact you want to make in the world.
Align your actions and decisions with your core values and passions.
Engage in Meaningful Work:
Seek careers or volunteer opportunities that align with your purpose and passions.

Strive for excellence and continuous improvement in your professional endeavors.
Adopt a Growth-Oriented Approach
Foster Meaningful Relationships
Build Strong Connections:
Invest time in building and nurturing relationships with family, friends, and your community.
Communicate openly and empathetically, and offer support and encouragement to others.
Seek Mutual Growth:
Surround yourself with people who challenge and inspire you to grow.
Engage in activities and discussions that promote mutual learning and development.
Pursue Passion and Purpose Identify Your Passion:
Reflect on what truly excites and motivates you.
Pursue hobbies and activities that bring joy and fulfillment.
Align with Your Purpose:
Set goals that align with your values and long-term vision.
Engage in work or volunteer opportunities
that contribute to your sense of purpose
Cultivate Continuous Learning Adopt a Lifelong Learning Attitude:
Stay curious and open to new experiences and knowledge.
Take courses, read books, and seek out mentors to expand your skills and understanding.
Embrace Challenges and Feedback:
View challenges as opportunities to learn and grow.
Actively seek feedback and use it constructively to improve yourself.
Practice Financial Wisdom Manage Finances Responsibly:
Create and stick to a budget that allows for saving and investing in your future.
Avoid unnecessary debt and make informed financial decisions.
Invest in Experiences:

Spend money on experiences that enrich your life and create lasting memories.
Balance financial security with enjoying the present.
Give Back and Contribute Volunteer and Support Causes:
Find causes that resonate with you and volunteer your time or resources.
Contribute to your community and help those in need.
Mentor and Inspire:
Share your knowledge and experiences to help others grow.
Encourage and support the aspirations and development of those around you.
Balance Work and Play Set Boundaries:
Establish clear boundaries between work and personal time to ensure a healthy work-life balance.
Prioritize time for relaxation and leisure activities that you enjoy.
Engage in Hobbies:
Dedicate time to hobbies and interests that bring you joy and relaxation.
Explore new activities that stimulate your creativity and passion.

Reflect and Adjust Regular Self-Reflection:
Take time to reflect on your goals, progress, and areas for improvement. Celebrate your achievements and learn from your experiences.
Adapt and Grow:
Be open to adjusting your plans and strategies as needed.
Embrace change and stay flexible in your approach to living abundantly.

By integrating these principles into your life, you can cultivate a growth mindset while enjoying a fulfilling, abundant life.

This holistic approach ensures that you are continually growing, learning, and contributing positively to yourself and the world around you.

Chapter 15

Self Compassion While Maintaining a Growth Mindset

Self-compassion while maintaining a growth mindset involves balancing the understanding and kindness towards oneself with the motivation to learn and grow. Here are some key principles and actionable steps to integrate self- compassion with a growth mindset:
Understanding Self-Compassion Practice Self-Kindness:
Treat yourself with the same kindness and understanding you would offer to a friend.
Be gentle with yourself during times of failure or when you make mistakes.
Acknowledge Common Humanity:
Recognize that everyone experiences difficulties and setbacks; you are not alone. Understand that imperfection is part of the human experience.
Be Mindful of Your Emotions:
Observe your thoughts and feelings without judgment.

Allow yourself to experience emotions fully without suppressing or exaggerating them. Integrating Self-Compassion with a Growth Mindset
Embrace Imperfection as Part of Growth:
Accept that mistakes and failures are opportunities for learning and growth. View challenges as a natural part of the journey towards improvement.
Set Realistic and Compassionate Goals:

Set goals that are challenging yet attainable, considering your current abilities and resources.

Be patient with yourself as you work towards your goals, recognizing that progress takes time.

Actionable Steps

Develop a Compassionate Inner Dialogue:

Replace self-criticism with supportive and encouraging self-talk.

When you catch yourself being harsh, pause and reframe your thoughts more kindly.

Reflect on Personal Growth:

Regularly reflect on your progress and the lessons learned from both successes and failures.

Celebrate your achievements, no matter how small, and acknowledge the effort you put in.

Practice Self-Care:

Prioritize activities that nurture your well- being, such as exercise, hobbies, and relaxation.

Ensure you get adequate rest and manage stress through techniques like mindfulness or meditation.

Balancing Self-Compassion and Ambition Understand Your Limits:

Recognize when to push yourself and when to give yourself a break.

Avoid overworking and understand that rest and recovery are essential for long- term success.

Be Flexible with Your Plans:

Adapt your goals and strategies based on your experiences and changing circumstances.

Be open to adjusting your path while maintaining your overall vision and aspirations.

Mindful Practices for Self-Compassion and Growth Mindfulness Meditation:

Engage in mindfulness meditation to develop greater awareness and acceptance of your thoughts and emotions.

Use guided meditations that focus on self- compassion and growth.
Journaling:
Keep a journal to document your thoughts, feelings, and progress.
Reflect on your experiences, both positive and negative, and write about how you can grow from them.
Encourage Self-Compassion in Others Model Compassionate Behavior:
Demonstrate self-compassion in your actions and interactions.
Encourage others to be kind to themselves and to embrace a growth mindset.

Create a Supportive Environment:

Foster a culture where mistakes are viewed as learning opportunities. Provide support and encouragement to others in their personal growth journeys.
By integrating self-compassion with a growth mindset, you can maintain a healthy balance between striving for improvement and being kind to yourself.
This approach not only enhances your personal development but also promotes emotional well-being and resilience.

Chapter 16

Money Manifestation and a Growth MIndset

Money manifestation and a growth mindset can complement each other to create a powerful approach to financial success. By combining the principles of manifesting wealth with the attitudes and behaviors associated with a growth mindset, you can foster an environment conducive to achieving financial goals and personal development.
Principles of Money Manifestation Positive Affirmations:
Use positive affirmations to reframe your mindset around money. For example, "I am capable of achieving financial abundance" or "Money flows to me effortlessly." Visualization:
Visualize your financial goals in detail. Imagine the lifestyle, experiences, and security that come with financial abundance.
Create vision boards with images and symbols that represent your financial aspirations.
Gratitude:
Practice gratitude for the money you currently have, no matter the amount. This mindset attracts more abundance.
Regularly acknowledge and appreciate financial gains and opportunities.
Integrating a Growth Mindset Embrace Learning:
View financial education as a continuous journey. Take courses, read books, and seek out mentors to expand your financial knowledge.
Stay curious about different investment opportunities, saving strategies, and ways to diversify income.
Learn from Setbacks:
Treat financial setbacks and mistakes as learning experiences. Reflect on what went wrong and how to improve in the future.

Maintain resilience and adapt your strategies based on these lessons.

Set Incremental Goals:
Break down your financial aspirations into smaller, achievable milestones. Celebrate progress along the way.
Use SMART goals (Specific, Measurable, Achievable, Relevant, Time-bound) to create a clear path to financial success.
Actionable Steps for Money Manifestation with a Growth Mindset
Develop a Financial Plan:
Create a detailed financial plan that includes budgeting, saving, investing, and debt management.
Regularly review and adjust your plan based on your evolving financial situation and goals.
Invest in Yourself:
Allocate resources for personal and professional development, such as education, certifications, and skill-building.
Recognize that investing in yourself can lead to greater earning potential and financial stability.
Practice Financial Discipline:
Cultivate habits that support long-term financial health, such as regular saving, prudent spending, and avoiding unnecessary debt.
Use tools and apps to track expenses, monitor investments, and manage your budget effectively.
Network and Collaborate:
Connect with like-minded individuals who share your financial goals and can offer support, advice, and opportunities.
Join financial clubs, attend workshops, and participate in online forums to expand your network.
Stay Flexible and Adaptable:
Be open to adjusting your financial strategies as you learn and grow.
Stay informed about market trends and economic changes.

Diversify your income streams to reduce risk and increase financial security.

Mindful Practices for Manifestation and Growth

Daily Affirmations and Visualization:

Incorporate daily affirmations and visualization practices into your routine. Spend a few minutes each day focusing on your financial goals and imagining achieving them.

Use meditation to clear your mind and focus on your financial intentions.

Gratitude Journaling:

Keep a gratitude journal specifically for financial blessings. Write down any financial gains, opportunities, and positive money-related experiences.

Reflect on how these experiences contribute to your overall financial grow

Reflective Journaling:

Maintain a journal to document your financial journey, including goals, setbacks, lessons learned, and progress.

Regularly review your entries to gain insights and identify patterns that can inform your future financial strategies. Encouraging Financial Growth in Others Share Knowledge and Experiences:

Offer guidance and support to others who are seeking to improve their financial situation.

Share resources, tools, and strategies that have helped you on your financial journey.

Promote a Growth-Oriented Financial Culture:

Foster an environment where discussions about money are open, supportive, and focused on growth and learning.

Encourage others to view financial challenges as opportunities for development and to adopt a proactive approach to financial management.

By combining money manifestation techniques with a growth mindset, you can create a comprehensive approach to achieving financial abundance. This blend of positive thinking, continuous learning, and practical financial management can lead to sustainable financial success and personal fulfillment.

Chapter 17

Create Your Life Vision by Having a Growth Mindset

Creating a life vision with a growth mindset involves setting a dynamic, evolving roadmap for your future that emphasizes continuous learning, resilience, and personal development. Here are some steps and strategies to help you craft a compelling life vision while maintaining a growth mindset:

Steps to Create Your Life Vision Reflect on Your Core Values and Passions

Identify Your Values: Write down the core values that drive your decisions and behaviors (e.g., integrity, creativity, compassion). Discover Your Passions: Reflect on activities and topics that energize and excite you. Consider what you would pursue if time and resources were unlimited.
Set Long-Term Goals
Define Your Aspirations: Think about where you want to be in 5, 10, or 20 years.
Envision your ideal career, relationships, health, and lifestyle. Break Down Goals: Divide long-term goals into manageable short-term milestones.
Use the SMART criteria (Specific, Measurable, Achievable, Relevant, Time- bound) to clarify your objectives.
Embrace a Growth Mindset

Adopt a Learning Attitude: View challenges and failures as opportunities to learn and grow. Commit to lifelong learning and skill development.

Cultivate Resilience: Develop strategies to bounce back from setbacks. Embrace change and be adaptable in your approach to achieving your vision.

Visualize Your Success

Create a Vision Board: Gather images, quotes, and symbols that represent your goals and aspirations. Place them on a board where you can see them daily. Practice Daily Visualization: Spend a few minutes each day visualizing yourself achieving your goals. Imagine the feelings and benefits associated with your success.

Develop an Action Plan

Outline Steps: Identify specific actions you need to take to reach your milestones. Create a timeline to track your progress.

Seek Resources and Support: Identify the resources, knowledge, and people that can help you. Network with mentors, join relevant communities, and access educational materials.

**Stay Flexible and

Adapt

Monitor Progress: Regularly review your goals and adjust your plans as needed. Be open to changing direction based on new information and experiences.

Celebrate Small Wins: Acknowledge and celebrate progress, no matter how small.

Recognize your achievements and the effort you've invested.

Envision Your Ideal Future

Create a Detailed Vision:

Imagine your life in 5, 10, or 20 years.

Where do you live? What kind of work do you do? What relationships do you have?

How do you spend your time?
Write a vivid description of your ideal future, including all aspects of your life: career, family, health, hobbies, and personal development.
Use Visualization Techniques:
Spend time each day visualizing your ideal life. Picture yourself achieving your goals and living according to your values.
Create a vision board with images and words that represent your aspirations and

Set SMART Goals

Specific, Measurable, Achievable, Relevant, Time-bound (SMART) Goals:

Break down your life vision into specific, actionable goals.

Ensure each goal is clear, measurable, realistic, relevant to your vision, and has a defined timeline.

Create Short-term and Long-term Goals:

Develop a mix of short-term goals (within a year) and long-term goals (5+ years) that align with your vision.

Regularly review and adjust these goals as needed to stay on track and accommodate changes in your life.

Reflect and Revise Regular Reflection:

Set aside regular times to reflect on your progress, celebrate successes, and identify areas for improvement.

Use reflection to stay aligned with your vision and make necessary adjustments.

Revise Your Vision as Needed:

Understand that your life vision may evolve over time. Be flexible and open to redefining your goals and aspirations as you grow.

Periodically revisit your vision statement and make revisions to ensure it continues to reflect your true desires and values.

By integrating these steps and principles, you can create a life vision that is dynamic, fulfilling, and aligned with a growth mindset. This approach will help you stay motivated, resilient, and continually progressing towards a life that reflects your deepest values and aspirations.

Chapter 18

My Purpose With a Growth Mindset

Define Your Core Values and Purpose Identify Your Core Values:
Reflect on what is most important to you in life, such as integrity, creativity, freedom, or compassion.
Write down your core values and consider how they influence your decisions and goals.
Clarify Your Life Purpose:
Think about what drives you and gives your life meaning. This could be related to your career, relationships, personal growth, or contributions to society.
Craft a personal mission statement that encapsulates your purpose and values

Finding your purpose in life while maintaining a growth mindset involves a continuous journey of self-discovery, learning, and adaptation. Here are some steps to help you identify and live your purpose with a growth-oriented approach:
Self-Discovery and Reflection Identify Your Passions:
Reflect on what activities and topics ignite your enthusiasm and joy. Consider what you love doing in your free time and what activities make you lose track of time.
Recognize Your Strengths:
Take note of your natural talents and skills. What do others often compliment you on? Consider taking personality and strengths assessments to gain further insights.
Reflect on Past Experiences:
Look back at your life experiences to identify moments when you felt most fulfilled and successful.
Think about the challenges you've overcome and the lessons learned.

Define Your Values:
Clarify what principles and values are most important to you. These could be integrity, compassion, creativity, etc.
Ensure your purpose aligns with your core values.

Setting a Purpose Craft a Purpose Statement:

Create a clear and concise statement that defines your life's purpose.
This should reflect your passions, strengths, and values.
Example: "My purpose is to inspire and empower others through creative expression and continuous learning."
Align with Your Goals:
Set long-term and short-term goals that align with your purpose.
Ensure these goals are specific, measurable, achievable, relevant, and time-bound (SMART).
Cultivating a Growth Mindset Embrace Challenges:
View obstacles as opportunities to grow and learn rather than setbacks.
Develop resilience by tackling challenges head-on and learning from each experience.
Seek Continuous Improvement:
Commit to lifelong learning. Stay curious and seek new knowledge and skills that align with your purpose.
Attend workshops, read books, and engage in activities that promote personal and professional growth.

Learn from Feedback:
Actively seek constructive feedback and use it to improve yourself.
View criticism as a tool for growth rather than a personal attack.
Celebrate Effort and Progress:

Focus on the effort you put into achieving your goals rather than just the outcomes. Celebrate small victories and milestones to stay motivated and encouraged.

Practical Implementation Develop an Action Plan:
Break down your purpose into actionable steps. Create a plan that includes specific actions, timelines, and resources needed. Prioritize tasks and set deadlines to stay organized and focused.

Track Your Progress:
Use tools like journals, apps, or spreadsheets to monitor your progress towards your goals.

Regularly review your achievements and adjust your plan as necessary.

Stay Accountable:
Share your purpose and goals with a trusted friend, mentor, or coach who can offer support and hold you accountable. Join groups or communities with similar aspirations for mutual encouragement and accountability.

Balancing Purpose and Well-being Maintain Work-Life Balance:
Ensure that pursuing your purpose does not come at the expense of your health and well-being.

Schedule time for relaxation, hobbies, and relationships to maintain a balanced life.

Practice Self-Compassion:
Be kind to yourself, especially when facing setbacks or challenges.

Recognize that growth and fulfillment are processes that require time and patience.

Reflect and Adapt Regular Reflection:
Set aside regular times to reflect on your progress, celebrate successes, and identify areas for improvement.

Use reflection to stay aligned with your purpose and make necessary adjustments.

Adapt and Evolve:

Understand that your purpose may evolve over time. Be flexible and open to redefining your goals and aspirations as you grow. Periodically revisit your purpose statement and make revisions to ensure it continues to reflect your true desires and values.
By following these steps, you can identify your purpose in life and live it fully with a growth mindset. This approach will help you stay motivated, resilient, and continually progressing towards a life that reflects your deepest values and aspirations.

Chapter 19

My Legacy By Having a Growth Mindset

67

Creating a legacy through the lens of a growth mindset involves shaping a lasting impact that reflects continuous learning, resilience, and positive influence on others. Here are steps and principles to help you build a meaningful legacy rooted in a growth mindset:

Define Your Legacy Vision Clarify Your Core Values and Beliefs:

Reflect on the values and principles that are most important to you. Consider how these values guide your actions and decisions.
Envision Your Impact:
Think about how you want to be remembered and the impact you want to have on your family, community, and the world.
Write down your vision for your legacy, encompassing personal, professional, and social aspects.

Set Growth-Oriented Goals Identify Long-term Goals:
Set ambitious but realistic long-term goals that align with your legacy vision.
Break down these goals into smaller, manageable steps to make them achievable.
Adopt a Learning and Development Plan:
Commit to continuous learning and self- improvement in areas that contribute to your legacy.
Engage in activities like reading, taking courses, and seeking mentorship to develop new skills and knowledge.

Cultivate Key Qualities Resilience and Adaptability:
Embrace challenges and setbacks as opportunities to grow and improve.
Develop strategies to bounce back from failures and remain adaptable to change.
Empathy and Compassion:
Foster empathy and compassion in your interactions with others.
Strive to understand and support others, contributing to a positive and nurturing environment.
Integrity and Authenticity:
Maintain integrity in your actions and decisions, staying true to your values.
Be authentic in your relationships and pursuits, ensuring that your legacy reflects your true self.
Inspire and Mentor Others Lead by Example:
Demonstrate a growth mindset in your daily life by continuously learning, adapting, and improving.
Show others the benefits of a growth mindset through your actions and achievements.
Mentor and Support:

Share your knowledge and experiences to help others grow and achieve their potential.
Offer guidance, encouragement, and resources to those who seek your mentorship.
Foster a Growth-Oriented Culture:
Encourage a culture of continuous learning and improvement in your community or organization.
Recognize and celebrate efforts and progress, not just outcomes.

Build Lasting Contributions Create Positive Change:
Identify areas where you can make a significant impact, whether it's through community service, innovation, or advocacy.
Work on projects and initiatives that address these areas and create lasting positive change.
Leave a Tangible Legacy:
Consider ways to leave a tangible legacy, such as writing a book, establishing a foundation, or creating a scholarship fund.
Ensure that these contributions align with your values and vision for your legacy.
Reflect and Evolve Regular Self-Reflection:
Set aside time regularly to reflect on your progress towards your legacy goals.
Evaluate your actions and decisions to ensure they align with your vision and values.
Adapt and Grow:
Be open to evolving your legacy vision as you grow and learn. Your understanding of what you want to leave behind may change over time.
Continuously seek new ways to enhance your impact and contribution.
Practical Steps to Implement Your Legacy Vision

Document Your Vision and Goals:
Write down your legacy vision and the goals you aim to achieve.
Create an action plan with specific steps, timelines, and milestones.
Share Your Vision:
Communicate your legacy vision with family, friends, and colleagues to garner support and accountability.
Encourage others to join you in your efforts, fostering a collective impact.
Track Your Progress:
Use journals, apps, or other tools to monitor your progress and reflect on your journey.
Regularly review and adjust your goals and strategies as needed to stay on track.
By integrating these principles and steps, you can create a legacy that embodies a growth mindset. This approach ensures that your impact is meaningful, dynamic, and continually evolving, leaving a lasting impression that inspires others to adopt a growth-oriented perspective.

Chapter 20

Growth Mindset for Women

Cultivating a growth mindset can be particularly empowering for women, offering a pathway to overcome challenges, embrace opportunities, and achieve personal and professional success. Here are specific strategies and principles tailored to help women develop and maintain a growth mindset:
Understand the Growth Mindset Definition and Importance:
A growth mindset is the belief that abilities and intelligence can be developed through dedication, effort, and learning.
Recognize that embracing a growth mindset leads to resilience, innovation, and
continuous improvement.

Challenge Fixed Mindset Thoughts:

Be aware of fixed mindset thoughts that suggest abilities are static ("I'm just not good at math").
Replace them with growth mindset affirmations ("I can improve my math skills with practice and effort").
Embrace Continuous Learning Invest in Education and Skills:
Pursue educational opportunities, courses, and workshops to enhance your knowledge and skills.
Stay updated with trends and advancements in your field to remain competitive and informed.
Seek Feedback and Act on It:

Actively seek constructive feedback from mentors, colleagues, and peers.

Use feedback as a tool for growth rather than a critique of your abilities.

Build Resilience and Overcome Challenges View Challenges as Opportunities:

Approach challenges with curiosity and a problem-solving attitude.
Understand that setbacks are part of the growth process and use them as learning experiences.
Develop Resilience:
Cultivate resilience by practicing stress management techniques such as mindfulness, meditation, and exercise.
Surround yourself with a supportive network of friends, family, and mentors who encourage and uplift you.
Foster Self-Compassion and Confidence Practice Self-Compassion:
Be kind to yourself, especially when facing difficulties or failures.
Recognize that everyone makes mistakes and that these moments are opportunities to learn and grow.
Build Self-Confidence:
Celebrate your achievements, no matter how small, to build confidence and reinforce a positive self-image.
Set realistic, achievable goals and acknowledge your progress towards them.
Empowerment Through Networking and Mentorship
Find Mentors and Role Models:
Seek out mentors who inspire you and can provide guidance and support.
Learn from their experiences and apply their insights to your own journey.
Build a Supportive Network:
Connect with other women who share your aspirations and values.

Join professional organizations, attend networking events, and participate in online communities to build relationships and share resources.
Challenge Gender Stereotypes and Bias Acknowledge and Address Bias:
Be aware of gender biases and stereotypes that may impact your self-perception and opportunities.
Advocate for yourself and others by challenging these biases and promoting equity in the workplace and beyond.
Promote Inclusivity:
Support and mentor other women to create a culture of inclusivity and empowerment.
Encourage diverse perspectives and voices in all areas of your life, from professional settings to community involvement.
Set Ambitious Yet Realistic Goals Define Your Goals:
Set clear, ambitious goals that align with your values and aspirations.
Break these goals into smaller, manageable steps to make them achievable.
Create an Action Plan:
Develop a detailed plan for reaching your goals, including specific actions, timelines, and milestones.
Regularly review and adjust your plan as needed to stay on track and adapt to changes.

Advocate for Yourself Communicate Your Needs and Desires:

Clearly articulate your goals, needs, and desires in both personal and professional settings.
Practice assertive communication to advocate for yourself effectively.
Seek Opportunities for Advancement:
Look for opportunities for career advancement, such as promotions, new projects, and leadership roles.
Be proactive in seeking out these opportunities and demonstrating your readiness for them
Reflect and Adapt Regular Self-Reflection:
Set aside time regularly to reflect on your progress, celebrate successes, and identify areas for improvement.
Use reflection to stay aligned with your goals and values.
Adapt and Evolve:
Be open to evolving your goals and strategies as you grow and learn.
Embrace change and be willing to adjust your path to better align with your evolving aspirations and circumstances.
By integrating these strategies and principles, women can cultivate a growth mindset that empowers them to overcome challenges, embrace opportunities, and achieve their full potential. This approach fosters resilience, continuous learning, and a supportive community, creating a foundation for lasting success and fulfillment.

Chapter 21

Growth Mindset for Men

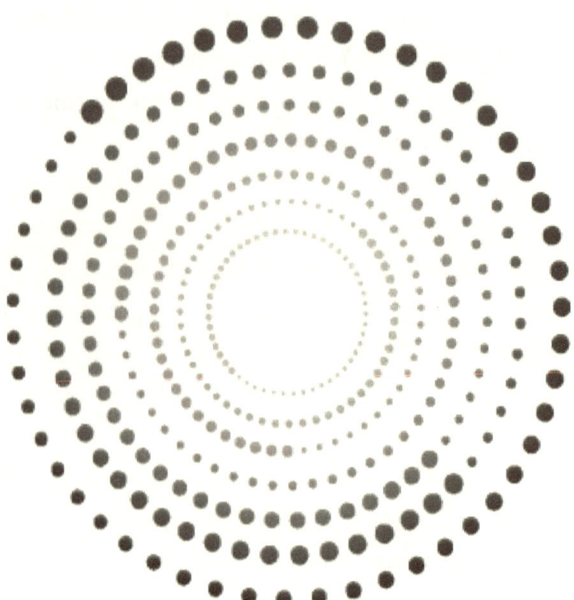

Absolutely, the principles of a growth mindset are applicable to everyone, regardless of gender. Here's how men can cultivate a growth mindset:

Embrace Challenges and Effort View Challenges as Opportunities: Approach challenges with a mindset of curiosity and resilience, seeing them as opportunities for growth rather than threats to your abilities. Embrace difficult tasks as chances to learn and improve, rather than shying away from them.

Value Effort and Persistence:

Recognize that effort and perseverance are key components of success. Embrace a "never give up" attitude, understanding that setbacks are natural and part of the learning process

Learn and Adapt Continuously Seek Learning Opportunities:
Actively seek out opportunities to learn and acquire new skills,
whether through formal education, workshops, or self- directed
learning.
Stay curious and open-minded, recognizing that there's always more to
discover and understand.
Adapt to Feedback:
Welcome constructive feedback as a valuable tool for growth and
improvement.
Use feedback to identify areas for development and adjust your
approach accordingly.

Foster Resilience and Overcome Setbacks Develop Resilience:
Cultivate resilience by building coping mechanisms to bounce back from setbacks.
Focus on solutions rather than dwelling on problems, using setbacks as opportunities to learn and grow stronger.
Maintain a Positive Outlook:
Foster optimism and positivity, even in the face of challenges.
Practice gratitude and focus on the progress you've made rather than dwelling on setbacks.

Cultivate Self-Compassion and Confidence Practice
Self-Compassion:
Be kind to yourself, especially during difficult times.
Treat yourself with the same understanding and empathy that you
would offer to a friend facing similar challenges.
Build Self-Confidence:
Celebrate your successes and acknowledge your strengths and
achievements.
Set realistic yet ambitious goals, pushing yourself outside your comfort
zone to foster personal growth.

Seek Mentorship and Support Find Mentors and Role Models:
Seek out mentors who can offer guidance, support, and wisdom based
on their own experiences.
Learn from the successes and failures of those who have walked similar
paths before you.
Connect with a Supportive Community:
Surround yourself with like-minded individuals who share your values
and aspirations.
Join networking groups, clubs, or organizations where you can
exchange ideas, offer support, and receive encouragement.

Advocate for Yourself and Others Communicate Your Goals and
Needs:
Clearly articulate your goals, needs, and desires in both personal and
professional settings.
Advocate for yourself confidently and assertively, ensuring that your
voice is heard and your contributions are recognized.
Support Gender Equity and Inclusivity:

Champion gender equity and inclusivity in all aspects of life, advocating for equal opportunities and treatment for all individuals. Use your platform and influence to promote diversity and inclusion in your workplace, community, and beyond.

Set Goals and Take Action Set Clear, Achievable Goals:
Define your goals clearly and break them down into actionable steps.
Set both short-term and long-term objectives, giving yourself
direction and purpose.
Take Consistent Action:
Commit to taking consistent, focused action towards your goals.
Stay disciplined and accountable, holding yourself accountable for
your progress and results.
Reflect and Adapt Regular Self-Reflection:
Set aside time regularly to reflect on your progress, celebrate your
successes, and identify areas for improvement.
Use reflection as an opportunity to course- correct and adjust your
approach as needed.
Embrace Change and Growth:
Embrace change as a natural part of life and growth.
Be willing to adapt and evolve, remaining flexible and open-minded in
your pursuit of personal and professional development.
By embodying these principles of a growth mindset, men can cultivate
resilience, adaptability, and continuous learning, empowering
themselves to overcome challenges, achieve success, and lead fulfilling
lives.

Chapter 22

Workbook: Cultivating a Growth Mindset

Section 1: Understanding the Growth Mindset

Questions:

What is the difference between a fixed mindset and a growth mindset?
How does having a growth mindset influence your approach to
challenges? List three characteristics of a growth mindset.
Why is it important to cultivate a growth mindset?

Answers:

A fixed mindset believes that abilities and intelligence are static, while
a growth mindset believes that they can be developed through
dedication and effort.

Having a growth mindset encourages you to see challenges as
opportunities for learning and growth rather than as threats to your
abilities.

Characteristics of a growth mindset include resilience in the face of
setbacks, a willingness to embrace challenges, and a belief in the power
of effort and persistence.

Cultivating a growth mindset is important because it leads to
resilience, innovation, and continuous improvement, ultimately
enabling individuals to achieve greater success and fulfillment.

Section 2: Embracing Challenges and Effort Questions:

How can you identify fixed mindset thoughts in yourself?
What strategies can you use to shift from a fixed mindset to a growth mindset when facing challenges?
Why is effort and persistence important in developing a growth mindset?
Provide an example of a challenge you've faced and how you approached it with a growth mindset.

Answers:
Fixed mindset thoughts often involve beliefs such as "I'm not good enough" or "I'll never be able to do this."
Strategies for shifting from a fixed mindset to a growth mindset include reframing challenges as opportunities for growth, seeking feedback and learning from mistakes, and focusing on the process rather than just the outcome.

Effort and persistence are important because they demonstrate a commitment to learning and improvement, even in the face of obstacles or setbacks.

Example answers will vary based on personal experiences. Encourage individuals to reflect on a specific challenge they've faced and how they approached it with a growth mindset, emphasizing the strategies they used to overcome obstacles and learn from the experience.

Building Resilience Questions:

What does resilience mean in the context of a growth mindset?

How can you cultivate resilience in the face of setbacks and challenges?

What are some coping strategies you can use to bounce back from setbacks?

How does maintaining a positive outlook contribute to resilience?

Answers:

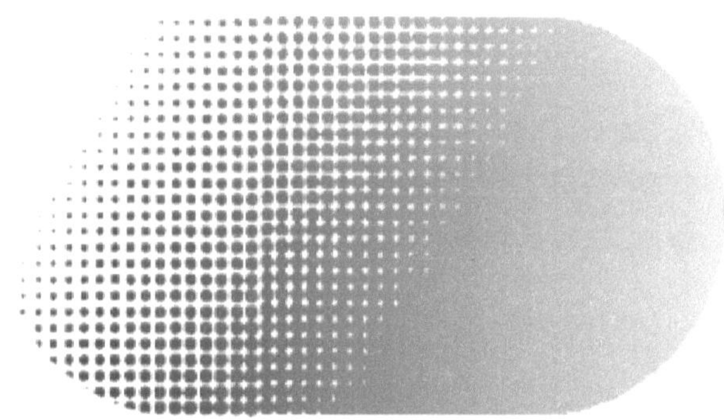

Answers:

Resilience in the context of a growth mindset refers to the ability to bounce back from setbacks, adapt to change, and persevere in the pursuit of goals despite obstacles.

You can cultivate resilience by reframing setbacks as opportunities for growth, focusing on solutions rather than dwelling on problems, and practicing self- compassion and acceptance.

Coping strategies for bouncing back from setbacks include seeking support from friends and family, practicing mindfulness and relaxation techniques, and breaking challenges into smaller, more manageable tasks.

Maintaining a positive outlook contributes to resilience by helping you see setbacks as temporary and surmountable, fostering optimism and hope even in difficult circumstances. By focusing on the progress you've made and expressing gratitude for what you have, you can bolster your resilience and navigate challenges more effectively.

Growth Mindset and Money Manifestation Questions:

How does a growth mindset influence one's approach to money manifestation?

What are some common fixed mindset beliefs about money, and how can they be reframed with a growth mindset?

How can practicing gratitude contribute to money manifestation?

What role does continuous learning and adaptation play in achieving financial abundance with a growth mindset?

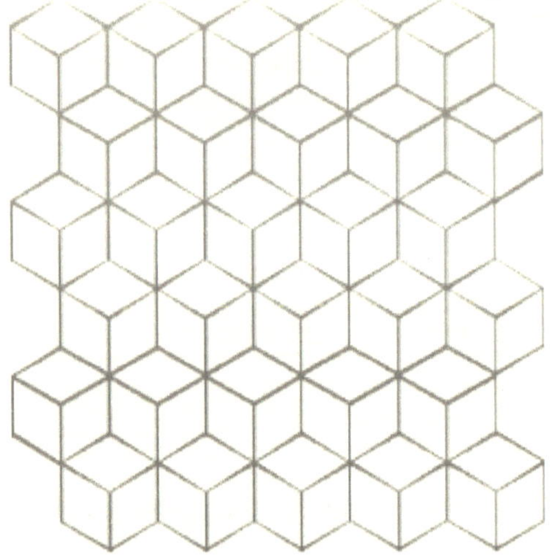

Answers:

A growth mindset influences one's approach to money manifestation by fostering a belief in abundance, resilience in the face of financial challenges, and a willingness to learn and adapt financial strategies. Common fixed mindset beliefs about money include "I'll never be wealthy," "Money is scarce," or "I'm not good with money." These beliefs can be reframed with a growth mindset by acknowledging that financial success is achievable through learning, effort, and perseverance.

Practicing gratitude contributes to money manifestation by shifting focus from scarcity to abundance. By expressing gratitude for what you already have, you create a positive mindset that attracts more opportunities for financial abundance.

Continuous learning and adaptation are essential for achieving financial abundance with a growth mindset because they enable individuals to stay informed about financial trends, explore new income opportunities, and adjust their financial strategies based on changing circumstances. By embracing a mindset of lifelong learning and flexibility, individuals can increase their financial literacy and resilience, ultimately manifesting greater wealth and prosperity.

Being a Changemaker with a Growth Mindset

Questions:

What does it mean to be a changemaker?

How does having a growth mindset contribute to being a changemaker?

What are some characteristics of changemakers with a growth mindset? How can individuals cultivate a growth mindset to become effective changemakers?

Answers:

Being a changemaker involves taking proactive steps to initiate positive change in one's community or society.

Changemakers seek to address social, environmental, or economic issues and inspire others to join in creating solutions.

Having a growth mindset contributes to being a changemaker by fostering resilience, adaptability, and a belief in the power of continuous learning and improvement. Changemakers with a growth mindset view obstacles as opportunities for growth and are willing to take risks and persevere in the face of challenges.

Characteristics of changemakers with a growth mindset include resilience in the face of setbacks, creativity in problem- solving, a willingness to challenge the status quo, and a commitment to lifelong learning and self-improvement.

Individuals can cultivate a growth mindset to become effective changemakers by reframing challenges as opportunities for growth, seeking feedback and learning from failure, maintaining a positive outlook, and fostering collaboration and innovation. By embracing a mindset of continuous learning and adaptation, individuals can overcome obstacles and drive positive change in their communities and beyond.

Having a Vision with a Growth Mindset Questions:
What does it mean to have a vision with a growth mindset?
How does a growth mindset influence the creation and pursuit of a vision?
What are the key components of a vision statement?
How can individuals align their goals and actions with their vision while maintaining a growth mindset?
Answers:
Having a vision with a growth mindset means envisioning a future that is dynamic, adaptable, and focused on continuous learning and improvement. It involves setting ambitious yet flexible goals and embracing challenges as opportunities for growth.
A growth mindset influences the creation and pursuit of a vision by fostering resilience, creativity, and a belief in the power of effort and perseverance.
Individuals with a growth mindset are more likely to see setbacks as temporary setbacks rather than insurmountable obstacles, allowing them to stay focused on their long-term vision.
The key components of a vision statement include a clear description of the desired future state, the values and principles guiding the vision, and the impact or contribution the vision aims to make. A vision statement should be inspiring, concise, and aligned with the individual's core values and aspirations.
Individuals can align their goals and actions with their vision while maintaining a growth mindset by setting SMART goals that are specific, measurable, achievable, relevant, and time-bound. They should regularly review and adjust their goals based on feedback and changing circumstances, remaining open to new opportunities and approaches for achieving their vision. By embracing a mindset of continuous learning and adaptation, individuals can stay resilient and focused on realizing their long-term vision.

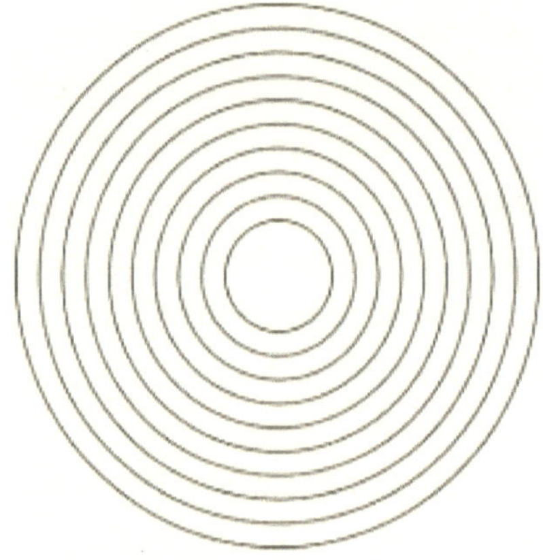

Self-Compassion While Maintaining a Growth Mindset
Questions:
What is self-compassion, and how does it relate to having a growth mindset?
Why is self-compassion important for personal growth and development? How can individuals practice self-compassion while striving for improvement and growth?
What are some strategies for cultivating self-compassion in the face of setbacks or failures?

Answers:
Self-compassion involves treating oneself with kindness, understanding, and acceptance, especially in times of difficulty or failure. It relates to having a growth mindset by providing a supportive foundation for learning and resilience, allowing individuals to embrace challenges and setbacks without harsh self-judgment. Self-compassion is important for personal growth and development because it fosters resilience, motivation, and emotional well-being. By offering ourselves the same care and understanding that we would offer to a friend, we create a nurturing environment that encourages learning, exploration, and self- improvement.

Individuals can practice self-compassion while striving for improvement and growth by cultivating mindfulness, acknowledging their humanity and imperfections, and reframing self-critical thoughts with kindness and understanding. They can also practice self-care and self-soothing techniques, such as deep breathing, meditation, or engaging in activities they enjoy.
Strategies for cultivating self-compassion in the face of setbacks or failures include recognizing that failure is a natural part of the learning process, reframing setbacks as opportunities for growth, and offering oneself words of encouragement and support. It's also helpful to remind oneself that everyone experiences challenges and setbacks, and that these experiences do not diminish one's worth or potential for growth.
Creating a Legacy with a Growth Mindset Questions:
What does it mean to create a legacy with a growth mindset?
How does having a growth mindset influence the impact and longevity of one's legacy?
What are some characteristics of legacies created with a growth mindset?

How can individuals cultivate a growth mindset to create a
meaningful and lasting legacy?

Answers:
Creating a legacy with a growth mindset involves leaving a positive
and lasting impact on the world through continuous learning,
resilience, and innovation. It means approaching life with a belief in
one's ability to grow and improve, both personally and professionally,
and using that mindset to make a difference in the lives of others.
Having a growth mindset influences the impact and longevity of one's
legacy by fostering adaptability, creativity, and a willingness to learn
from failure.
Individuals with a growth mindset are more likely to embrace
challenges, take risks, and persevere in the face of obstacles, ultimately
leaving a more significant and enduring mark on the world.

Characteristics of legacies created with a growth mindset include resilience in the face of setbacks, a commitment to lifelong learning and self-improvement, and a focus on empowering and inspiring others to reach their full potential. These legacies are often marked by innovation, collaboration, and a dedication to making a positive difference in the world.

Individuals can cultivate a growth mindset to create a meaningful and lasting legacy by reframing challenges as opportunities for growth, seeking feedback and learning from failure, and maintaining a positive outlook even in difficult circumstances.

They can also foster a culture of innovation and collaboration, encouraging others to embrace a growth mindset and join them in making a positive impact on the world.

Achieving Abundance with a Growth Mindset

Questions:

How does a growth mindset influence one's ability to achieve abundance?

What are some common limiting beliefs about abundance, and how can they be reframed with a growth mindset?

How does practicing gratitude contribute to manifesting abundance?

What role does continuous learning and adaptation play in achieving financial or personal abundance with a growth mindset?

Answers:

A growth mindset influences one's ability to achieve abundance by fostering resilience, creativity, and a belief in the power of continuous learning and improvement. Individuals with a growth mindset are more likely to see opportunities where others see obstacles and are willing to take risks and persevere in the face of challenges. Common limiting beliefs about abundance include "There's not enough to go around," "I'll never be wealthy," or "Money is the root of all evil." These beliefs can be reframed with a growth mindset by recognizing that abundance is not limited and that financial success is achievable through learning, effort, and perseverance.

Practicing gratitude contributes to manifesting abundance by shifting focus from scarcity to abundance. By expressing gratitude for what you already have, you create a positive mindset that attracts more opportunities for financial or personal abundance.

Continuous learning and adaptation are essential for achieving abundance with a growth mindset because they enable individuals to stay informed about opportunities, explore new possibilities, and adjust their strategies based on changing circumstances. By embracing a mindset of lifelong learning and flexibility, individuals can increase their resilience, creativity, and ultimately, their capacity for abundance.

Letting Go of a Fixed Mindset Questions:

What is a fixed mindset, and how does it differ from a growth mindset?

Why is it important to let go of a fixed mindset?

What are some common signs or beliefs associated with a fixed mindset?

How can individuals begin to shift from a fixed mindset to a growth mindset?

Answers:

A fixed mindset is the belief that abilities and intelligence are static traits that cannot be changed. In contrast, a growth mindset is the belief that abilities can be developed through dedication and effort. It's important to let go of a fixed mindset because it limits personal growth, stifles creativity, and hinders resilience. By embracing a growth mindset, individuals can unlock their full potential and achieve greater success and fulfillment.

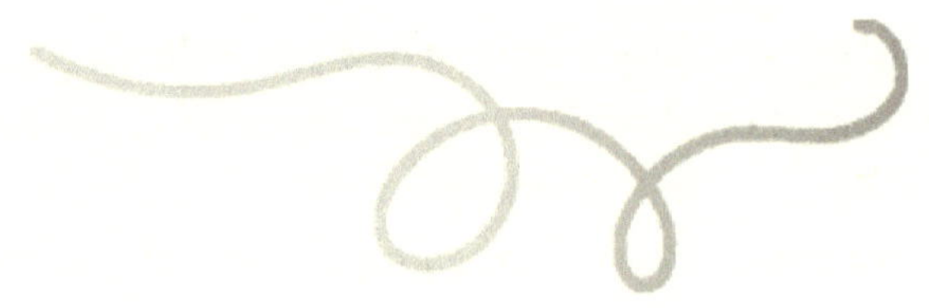

Common signs or beliefs associated with a fixed mindset include avoiding challenges, giving up easily in the face of obstacles, and viewing criticism as a personal attack rather than an opportunity for growth.

Fixed mindset individuals may also believe that talent alone leads to success and that effort is fruitless.

Individuals can begin to shift from a fixed mindset to a growth mindset by recognizing and acknowledging their fixed mindset beliefs, challenging these beliefs with evidence of growth and change, and adopting a mindset of curiosity, learning, and resilience. They can also seek out opportunities for growth, embrace challenges as opportunities for learning, and cultivate a positive and supportive inner dialogue.

: Changing Your Belief from Fixed to Growth Mindset
Questions:

What is the process of changing a belief from a fixed mindset to a growth mindset?

Why is it important to challenge and change fixed mindset beliefs?

What are some common barriers individuals face when transitioning to a growth mindset?

How can individuals cultivate a growth mindset and reinforce new beliefs over time?

Answers:
Changing a belief from a fixed mindset to a growth mindset involves recognizing and acknowledging fixed mindset beliefs, challenging them with evidence and alternative perspectives, and adopting new beliefs that emphasize the potential for growth and improvement. It's important to challenge and change fixed mindset beliefs because they limit personal growth, hinder resilience, and can lead to negative self-perceptions and behaviors. By adopting a growth mindset, individuals can unlock their full potential and achieve greater success and fulfillment.

Common barriers individuals face when transitioning to a growth mindset include fear of failure, self-doubt, and the discomfort of stepping outside of their comfort zone. Additionally, individuals may face resistance from others or societal norms that reinforce fixed mindset beliefs.

Individuals can cultivate a growth mindset and reinforce new beliefs over time by practicing self-awareness and mindfulness, seeking out challenges and learning opportunities, and surrounding themselves with supportive and growth-oriented individuals. They can also develop a growth mindset through consistent effort, perseverance, and a willingness to embrace setbacks and failures as opportunities for learning and growth.

Overcoming Limiting Beliefs While Maintaining a Growth Mindset
Questions:
What are limiting beliefs, and how do they impact one's ability to maintain a growth mindset?
Why is it important to identify and challenge limiting beliefs when striving for personal growth?
What are some common limiting beliefs that individuals may encounter while trying to maintain a growth mindset?
How can individuals overcome limiting beliefs and maintain a growth mindset in the face of challenges?
Answers:
Limiting beliefs are deeply ingrained thoughts or convictions that constrain individuals' potential and hinder their ability to maintain a growth mindset. They can create self-imposed barriers to growth, resilience, and personal development.
It's important to identify and challenge limiting beliefs when striving for personal growth because they can undermine efforts to cultivate a growth mindset, leading to self-doubt, fear of failure, and a reluctance to embrace challenges.
Common limiting beliefs that individuals may encounter while trying to maintain a growth mindset include "I'm not good enough," "I'll never succeed," or "I'm too old to change." These beliefs can stem from past experiences, societal norms, or negative self-talk.
Individuals can overcome limiting beliefs and maintain a growth mindset by practicing self-awareness and mindfulness, challenging negative thoughts with evidence and alternative perspectives, and reframing setbacks as opportunities for learning and growth. They can also seek support from mentors, coaches, or trusted friends and family members who can offer encouragement and perspective. Additionally, individuals can cultivate a positive and affirming inner dialogue, focusing on their strengths, achievements, and potential for growth.

Art Therapy Workbook_ Cultivating and Expanding a Growth Mindset

Art Therapy Lesson: Cultivating and Expanding a Growth Mindset
Lesson Overview
This art therapy lesson is designed to help participants understand, cultivate, and expand a growth mindset. The activities encourage self-reflection, visualization, and creative expression, which are key in developing a mindset that embraces challenges and sees failures as opportunities for growth.
Objectives
Understand the concept of a growth mindset.
Identify personal strengths and areas for growth.
Create a visual representation of personal growth.
Develop strategies to maintain and expand a growth mindset.
Materials Needed
Art supplies: colored pencils, markers, crayons, watercolor paints, brushes
Paper: various sizes, including large poster- sized paper
Magazines, scissors, and glue for collage- making
Inspirational quotes about growth mindset Journals or notebooks
Audio/visual equipment for playing soft background music (optional)
Duration 2 hours

Lesson Plan

• Introduction (10 minutes) Discussion: Start with a brief discussion about what a growth mindset is. Explain

that it's the belief that abilities and intelligence can be developed through dedication and hard work.
Examples: Share examples of growth mindset statements (e.g., "I can learn from my mistakes," "Challenges help me grow").

- Icebreaker Activity: My Growth Story (20 minutes)

Activity: Participants draw a timeline of their life highlighting key moments where they overcame challenges or learned something new.
Sharing: Allow volunteers to share their timelines with the group.

- Art Activity: Growth Tree (40 minutes) Instructions: Each participant draws a large tree on a piece of poster-sized paper. The tree should have strong roots, a trunk, and

branches.

Roots: Write or draw the foundational skills, strengths, and support systems they currently have.

Trunk: Illustrate their ongoing efforts and the actions they are taking to develop their skills.

Branches: Represent the goals and areas they want to grow in. They can add leaves or fruits with specific goals or aspirations. Materials: Use colored pencils, markers, and other available art supplies to make the tree vibrant and detailed.

- Reflection and Collage: Visualizing Growth (30 minutes)

Collage Creation: Provide magazines, scissors, and glue. Participants create a collage that represents what growth means to them. This can include images, words, and phrases that inspire a growth mindset. Journaling: While working on the collage, participants write down thoughts and feelings about growth and how they can cultivate a growth mindset in their journal.

• Group Sharing and Discussion (20 minutes)

Sharing: Participants share their Growth Trees and collages with the group, explaining the significance of the images and words they chose. Discussion: Facilitate a discussion about how visualizing growth can help maintain and expand a growth mindset. Encourage participants to share strategies they use to stay motivated and focused on growth.

• Conclusion and Takeaway (10 minutes)

Summary: Summarize key points about cultivating a growth mindset. Takeaway: Distribute a handout with growth mindset quotes and tips for maintaining a growth mindset. Closing: End with a positive affirmation or a brief mindfulness exercise to reinforce the concepts discussed.
Follow-Up Activities
Weekly Journaling: Encourage participants to keep a growth mindset journal, documenting challenges, learning experiences, and progress. Monthly Art Projects: Suggest monthly art projects that focus on different aspects of growth, such as resilience, creativity, and problem-solving.

Conclusion

It is never to late to start cultivating a growth spurt in your life at any age.

To expand your mind beyond its limits, is a extrordinary experience and change will take place and your world will expand into a effortless flow of life and abundance.

As i reflect back on my own story, I realize how many people dont get the help or advice they need at the moment of their trauma or situation and i had to learn and research on my own and pull from my own experiences to cultivate and grow my mindset and the way i percieve the world and change and go through pain to grow and many dark nights of the soul to start the healing process and trigger the spiral of life within me. And once you are on the other side it is a whole new world to navigate and find true happines in and acceptance of all you have been through and move forward into a new exsistance of sustainability and cultivation of the human soul and mind, body and spirit. And help others to follow the same growth.

Epilogue

Grow Expand Change Adapt

Lizette

Don't miss out!

Visit the website below and you can sign up to receive emails whenever Lizette publishes a new book. There's no charge and no obligation.

https://books2read.com/r/B-A-YIXOB-GPOMD

Connecting independent readers to independent writers.